what if i told you

21 Day Devotional

cory rice

tws | the writer's society publishing

To request permissions, contact TWS Publishing at www.thewriterssociety.online

Paperback ISBN 978-1-961180-19-2

TWS
The Writer's Society Publishing
Lodi, CA

Dedicated to the people of Hill City Church. Thank you for trusting and believing in me. I hope this devotional impacts your soul.

contents

A Word of Caution   vii

Daily Habits   xi

5 R's   xv

Day One   1
Mamba Mentality

Day Two   7
Whole

Day Three   11
Loved

Day Four   15
Unique

Day Five   19
Chosen

Day Six   23
Qualified

Day Seven   27
Worthy

Day Eight   31
Secured

Day Nine   35
Accepted

Day Ten   39
Valued

Day Eleven   43
Royal

Day Twelve   47
Forgiven

Day Thirteen   51
Blameless

Day Fourteen   55
Righteous

Day Fifteen   59
Known

Day Sixteen   63
Perfect

Day Seventeen   67
Masterpiece

Day Eighteen   71
Saint

Day Nineteen   75
Holy

Day Twenty   79
Victorious

Day Twenty One   83
Greatness

Last Challenge   87

About the Author   89
Also by Cory Rice   91

a word of caution

The theme for this devotional is Proverbs 23:7: "For as he thinks within himself, so he is." (NASB). How you think about yourself is the most important thinking you'll do.

A word of caution before you begin – this is a process... a journey... an adventure. You must embrace this process and be willing to do the work. Do not go through each day of this program casually. This type of work requires a mamba-like mentality (which I will explain in Day 1). It's important that you wrestle with the truths laid out in each day of this devotional. It's important that you confront how you think and speak to yourself. It's important to align and fearlessly proclaim what God has to say about you.

As you read this devotional, my goal isn't just to inspire you but to truly help you believe you matter. My goal is to help equip you with the truth of how God truly thinks and feels about you. However, do not make the assumption that confidence comes easy for me. You may only see me preach on a stage at Hill City Church or, listen to my podcast 2 *Pastors And A Mic*, or notice my life from what I post on socials. You may hear me speak or write with confidence on different subjects or believe I'm a very confident person. But like many of you, you don't get to see the struggle, the insecurities, the doubts, the tensions, the frustrations, the disappointments, the process. It can create this false dichotomy that I'm some kind of superhero faith pastor or dynamically confident person, and it's just not true. Confidence is a practice. Confidence is a daily declaration.

Confidence in Greek means to boldly proclaim what's in you. You've probably heard the following statement a hundred times, but it's so true – the same power that raised Jesus to life is the same power that lives in you. Reader – marinate and manifest that reality! True confidence means you can daringly claim you are already whole, loved, unique, chosen, qualified, worthy, secured, accepted, valued, royal, forgiven, blameless, righteous, known, perfect, a masterpiece, a saint, holy, victorious, and great. Depending on what you were taught in regard to Christianity, I know it may be uncomfortable for you to claim some of the words mentioned above. But don't be mad at these truths if they make you uncomfortable; be mad that you have believed limiting lies about yourself for far too long. All of these words are not given to you based on your behavior but are free gifts given because of Christ. Will you accept the truth? Your confidence hinges on it. These truths become a part of the private monologue within that will empower your public influence. Take inventory, then take responsibility. The world around us is full of chaos, but that does not mean your life has to be. The world needs you to stop playing small and to live in the fullness of who you truly are.

For those raised in the church and who have a hard time believing some of those words above are actually true about you, we're about to go on a 21-day adventure all around the truth of our identity. These truths are so important for us to understand because this is how confidence grows. As we partake in this 21-day challenge, you will soak in the truth of how your Father views you. We are going to practice falling in love with ourselves. Licensed mental health counselor Dr. Vassilia Binensztok reminds us this idea may be uncomfortable at first when she says, "When you're not used to being confident, confidence feels like arrogance. When you're used to being passive, assertiveness feels like aggression. When you're not used to getting your needs met, prioritizing yourself feels selfish. However, your comfort zone is not a good benchmark."

Many Church leaders have not set the body of Christ up for success in regard to proper confidence because they think it produces pride or encourages a lack of humility. **However, it's impossible for this message to produce pride because you're not the one who is earning these truths.** You are simply accepting them. Actually, the irony exposes that to reject these truths is prideful because it reveals your need and desire to work for and earn something that is already given. It reveals your attempt to try out for a position you already possess. It's your attempt at measuring up. This type of Christianity, is legalism and legalism is what leads to pride. As author C.S. Lewis says, "True humility is not thinking less of yourself, it's thinking of yourself less." Meaning you should have a high view of yourself because God has a high view of you! You are His most prized creation.

This devotional will help you recognize the power and freedom you already possess because of Jesus. This power and freedom, however, requires responsibility. Why is it important to recognize your responsibility? Because with power, you have the ability to either overpower or empower others. With freedom, you have the ability to either abuse it or flourish in it. The choice is yours, so choose wisely!

Disclaimer - THIS TAKES TIME, HARD WORK, AND CONSISTENCY. A lack of confidence is a bad habit that takes time to break. Scientifically, according to clinical and cognitive neuroscientist Dr. Caroline Leaf, it takes 63 days (or three cycles of 21 days. Which is why this devotional is 21 days) to break down a habit or pattern of thinking. It only takes one cycle of 21 days to break down a core habit and build a replacement one. (To avoid falling back into the habit or thought pattern, it's recommended to continue through two more cycles). It takes time to retrain your brain how to think about yourself. This work is not about intensity; it's about consistency. Consistently speaking God's truth into your soul.

Confidence also boosts when self-esteem and emotions are higher. Physical health and mental health play a huge part in this process as well. This devotional is about spiritual health, but if you're interested in a physical and mental health challenge, I've already released a free e-book titled *21 Days To Better Mental Health* that includes a 21-day meal plan and fitness challenge (you can find it on my website – saintsnotsinners.com). Becoming the best version of you will impact everyone in your household because everyone will reap the benefits of your mental, physical, and spiritual health.

Grab a journal and let's dive in!

daily habits

Every day for 21 days, you'll be going through some type of guided meditation. These daily habits are to help guide you through daily meditation after the devotional. These habits will help you train your thoughts around His permanent presence. Don't waste this season. It's time to create some healthy habits.

1. Focus on God's Faithfulness.

My confidence starts in His faithfulness. God will bring me through this season, just like He has every season before. It doesn't mean it will be without pain, hurt, or loss. It doesn't mean it will be easy. But I will grow through it if I decide to conquer the way I think. Will I have weak moments? Absolutely. But when I focus on His faithfulness, it allows gratitude to flow. When I am constantly rewiring my brain to think thankful thoughts, my perspective shifts. **A focus on His faithfulness won't always change the season. It will, however, change the way I experience it.**

Here are some ways I focus on God's faithfulness in my life:

- Journal. Write down your emotions and what's going on with your thought process. When it's written, you can go back later and see how God worked. If it's not written, it's not real. Start with a word to describe the week and go from there.
- Make a grateful list. Write down the things you are thankful for. My mother-in-law has a book designed for this sole purpose. She has thousands of entries… literally… because each thing she writes down is numbered.
- Make a worship playlist. Our church has done this for you on Spotify. You can make your own and add the songs you love that help shift your perspective.
- At meal times, before you dive into the food, each person has to share something they are thankful for, and it can't be the same as previous meals.

2. Embrace Slow Living.

Christian scholar Dallas Willard says, "Hurry is the great enemy of spiritual life in our day. You must ruthlessly eliminate hurry from your life." We won't be as effective in the Kingdom of God with a hurried soul. I challenge you to slow your routines, patterns, and schedules of busyness. When you look at the life of Jesus, He never did anything in a hurry. He even waits four days after the death of one of His best friends before He raises Lazarus from the dead. **Grace has a pace, and it is slow!**

Here are some ways I slow down:

- I sit on my back deck without my phone. I prefer earlier than later but pick your own time. Pick your time of day and beverage of choice (coffee, tea, wine, bourbon, etc.) and just pay attention to nature. Notice the trees, animals, flowers, grass, etc. Listen to the sounds around you. Take in the smells. Learn the art of sitting still.
- Schedule a time of the day when your kids/spouse get your full attention. This also means no phones for most of us. Create

a habit of playing with your loved ones without the distraction of texts, calls, or social media.

- Instead of movies on Netflix or scrolling mindlessly on social media, play a game, do a puzzle, build a fort, start a campfire, go on a walk/bike ride, etc. We have started a daily habit within our family where we go on a walk after dinner. It's becoming my favorite time of the day.
- I haven't done this yet, but I am planning on a day (most likely Friday since it is my day off) to turn off my phone the whole day. I hear this has been the greatest day of the week for the people I know who do this.

3. Fall in Love with You.

You will never be able to love others well or express God's peaceful, confident, and unshakable power if you still believe lies about you. You have to fall in love with yourself the way Jesus is in love with you. NEWS ALERT - He's not in love with a future version of you. You are blameless, worthy, and holy even though you sin and fall short because those three things aren't tied to your performance. They're tied to Jesus' performance. When you grasp this reality, it's impossible for it to produce pride because you didn't accomplish it. Jesus did on your behalf. **Therefore, you cannot be a dirty, wretched sinner and a beloved son or daughter of God at the same time. One is the Christian way of pretending to be humble; the other is your true identity.**

Here are some things to do or stop doing to fall in love with you:

- Conquer one negative thought. (We will talk through this at the end of Day 1.)
- Speak affirmation to yourself and create a personal motto. (We will talk through this at the end of Day 1.)
- Focus on your gifts. You are talented. You're not supposed to be a cheap imitation of someone else. Start walking in your

own gifts and watch God open doors for you that you thought would never be opened.

- Marinate in this question: "God, what are you trying to show me today about who you are and who I am?"
- Unfollow the people on social media that you find yourself comparing yourself to. It's often said, **"Confidence isn't walking into a room thinking you're better than everyone, it's walking in and not having to compare yourself to anyone at all."** (UNKNOWN AUTHOR)
- Start working out, eating right, and sleeping enough. Many mental and physical health issues are tied to these three. If you don't take the time to take care of yourself now, you'll have to make time for health issues later.
- Seek affirming relationships and share your emotions with safe people. You need other people in your life to help you process your feelings.
- Whatever you seek becomes tangible. Anything you give attention to grows (good or bad - that's why we speak only good). Write out the names of four people whose opinion of you actually matters. It's important to get the right people in your corner. Many people remember Muhammad Ali, but very few realize he had four men in his corner that he praises for his success – trainer Angelo Dundee, assistant trainer Wali Muhammad, physician Dr. Ferdie Pacheco, and assistant trainer/hype man Bundini Brown. Who are your four? I was recently watching the film Underrated (released in 2023) on Apple TV. It's a behind-the-scenes look at the life of 4x NBA Champion, 2x League MVP, and 1x NBA Finals MVP, Stephen Curry. In the movie, he reiterated the importance of the other 4 starters on his college basketball team at Davidson. He said, "I think about Jay Rich, Thomas, Max, and Boris (what they) all meant to me and my confidence as a player; you don't do anything in this life by yourself. You know, the confidence of the group is your superpower. And those four guys unlocked that for me." So again, who are your four?

5 r's

The 5 R's are how we consciously process a negative thought.

- Recognize a negative thought. What is something you find yourself saying to yourself? Bring it to the surface and write it out. If you never admit to the thought, you'll never be able to replace it.
- Release it. This will be a continual process. When you don't release it, you focus on it. When you focus on it, it doesn't lead to a change in action… it actually leads to repetition.
- Rewire your thinking. Write truth out on sticky notes or on your bathroom mirror. When you release a negative thought, you are rewiring how you think by replacing the negative thought with a positive one. Speak your identity found in Christ over your life every day. This is why you create a personal motto (see Day 1).
- Redevelop your habits. Write out your weekly schedule and goals. If it's not written, it's not real. Challenge yourself to be generous. Don't just have good intentions because your intentions mean nothing if you don't follow through. Set

reminders on your phone to be encouraging to others. You will have to put in some work to redevelop habits in your life, but your future self will thank you for it. Don't wait until New Year's. Do it now!

- Repeat the process while giving yourself grace.

day one

. . .

Mamba Mentality

WHAT IF I told you the only thing that separates you from being confident is the way you think?

I grew up in the suburbs of Detroit with three brothers and a love for sports, competition, and athletes. Hockey was and will always be my first love. My earliest memory of my love for the Detroit Red Wings happened in 1995 when I was eight-years old. I remember listening to them in the Stanley Cup Finals on the radio with my grandpa at his cottage in Northern Michigan. We were swept that year, but we would soon find glory, two years later and the Red Wings would go on to win back-to-back Cups. We ended up winning four Cups in an 11-year span from 1997-2008. During that time, we had 11 players who would end up in the NHL Hall of Fame.

At this stage in life, I also fell in love with boxing and basketball. I remember watching the Holyfield vs. Tyson II fight in 1997. You know, the one where Tyson bit Holyfield's ear off. It was awesome – but also traumatic. I guess Tyson was serious about all that eating people stuff.

If you know, you know. Basketball was a little safer, I'd say. Growing up a Michigan State fan, it was awesome to watch Mateen Cleaves and Mo Peterson bring Sparty Nation a National Championship in 2000. I'm also a faithful Detroit sports fan, so it was easy to fall in love with the bad boy Pistons 2.0 of 2004. I tried to grow my own Afro-style hair out to be like Ben Wallace. Of all these amazing players and teams, however, there was one person who stood out more than anyone else. At this time in my life, I really fell in love with the game of basketball because of Kobe Bryant. My first early memory was Kobe in the finals vs. Allen Iverson in 2001. Two guys I pretended to be in my basement, shooting on my Fisher Price basketball hoop. I have always said 'Kobe' every time I threw something into the trash can or heaved half-court shots in our church gym. He's an icon and will always be remembered because of his on-the-court greatness, intelligence, basketball IQ, and work ethic.

When I think of a confident athlete, the first person I think of is Kobe. Who do you think of? As I've aged, my favorite thing about Kobe Bryant was his mamba mentality. Mamba is his iconic nickname. As Kobe said, "To sum up what mamba mentality is, it means to be able to constantly try to be the best version of yourself. It's all about focusing on the process and trusting in the hard work when it matters most. Everything negative - pressure, challenges - is all an opportunity for me to rise. I have nothing in common with lazy people who blame others for their lack of success. Great things come from hard work and perseverance. No excuses." Kobe understood that legacy matters, but you will only live as long as your story is worthy of being told. Are you living in a way that impacts the people you have influence over? Kobe once said, "The most important thing is to try and inspire people so that they can be great in whatever they want to do." That is true Kingdom mentality. In fact, his character is revealed in the written piece by ESPN senior writer Ramona Shelburne when she writes, "I wanted to go last. To let everyone else write their stories on Kobe Bryant as he approached retirement and then top them all. It was an audacious gamble. But that was my pitch to him in the winter of 2016.

I thought the audacity would appeal to him. He'd admire the confidence, the swagger, maybe even chuckle at the arrogance. Nope. He said he'd do a story with me about his life, but not out of vanity – mine or his. 'I'm not interested in self-serving pieces,' he said bluntly. 'It has to be something where an athlete reads it and is inspired by something, learns something and pushes themselves.'" This is why I love Kobe. He had this killer instinct to rise to the occasion. Yet, people hated on what they thought was arrogance. However, don't be misled; there's a major difference between confidence and arrogance. People who don't know you will confuse the two.

After Kobe's death in 2020, I purchased a jersey from the Mamba Sports Academy because I love what mamba stands for. Hard work requires discipline. Hard work is contagious. Hard work is what it takes to change the way you think. That is what this devotional is all about.

Although I loved Kobe's confidence and approach to sports, it's important to note that confidence is not found in your own abilities or qualities. It's not found in your appearance, accomplishments, intelligence, or talents. Those all fade. **True confidence grows when you begin to love yourself the way your Creator does.** I'm unqualified to tell you how to live or what to believe. I am, however, qualified to tell you how loved you are. You will never love yourself well if you don't know how loved you are. When you believe what your Creator says about you, no person or circumstance can change that.

So, welcome to the beginning of a new you.

Today's Work

1. Conquer one negative thought. What is something you find yourself saying to yourself? (I'm not good enough, attractive enough, smart enough, etc.). Write it out below or in your journal. If you never admit to the thought, you'll never be able to replace it. Therefore, it will always have subconscious power over you. Remember, you can't always control the thoughts you have, but you can control the thoughts you hold onto. How? The 5 R's (refer back to the 5 R's page for a more in-depth explanation of the following). These 5 R's work hand in hand with conquering a negative thought.

- Recognize your negative thought.
- Release it.
- Rewire your thinking.
- Redevelop your habits.
- Repeat the process while giving yourself grace.

2. Speak affirmation to yourself and create a personal motto. We will repeat it every day in this devotional. Think success. Think peace. Think joy. Think healing. Always start your day with positive self-talk. You owe it to yourself. This can be anything you need to speak over your life to help you rewire the way you think about God and the way He thinks about you. This is a practical way to renew your mind. It's time to challenge yourself to believe the best about yourself. An incredible example of a personal motto happened within the leadership team on the island of Aruba. In 2010, perceived crime affected tourism negatively (remember the publicity around Natalee Holloway?). Of all the Caribbean islands, Aruba was the worst off financially. They decided to create a motto – ONE HAPPY ISLAND. By 2013, Aruba became one of the safest islands in the Caribbean as tourist rates hit an all-time high. Talk about the power of words!

As you create a personal motto, you will repeat this daily during this devotional. Write it on your mirror, car dash, phone homepage, or sticky notes. If you do not have any confidence in private, you won't live with any confidence in public. My motto is this: "I love me. I am whole and perfect as I was created. I belong. I matter. I am not my body. I am not my accumulations. I am not my achievements. I am not my reputation."

Here are examples of other real people who have created a personal motto:

- "I'm ready to go to the next level. I can do hard things. I won't settle for less than what I deserve."
- "I am not defined by my actions. I am not defined by my feelings. I am in Christ so today, I can love like Christ. God is proud of me!"
- "Don't sweat the small stuff. I am good enough. I am beautiful. I am lovable. I am strong."
- "I'm a confident son of the Almighty God and He smiles at me."
- "Today, I'm going to lean into my Father and not my fears."
- "God is proud of me because He made me. He trusts me."
- "I'm God's favorite and He delights in me."

day two

. . .

Whole

WHAT IF I told you you're whole – made in His image and likeness?

YOU'RE NOT BROKEN!

How you think about yourself is the most important thinking you will do. The only time you live broken is when you believe this lie about who you are. **If you believe you're broken, you'll live broken.** Clinical psychologist Dr. Nicole LePera says it this way, "Broken is the illusion created by trauma. Wholeness is the truth." Trauma is not what happened to you; it's what happened inside of you (your internal psychological wound) because of what happened to you. Trauma disconnects you from your true self and feeds you lies about who you are. We all have trauma, and I believe we all need to talk about it with safe people. <u>Hurt must be heard before it can be healed.</u> Healing is not about fixing yourself; it's really about discovering yourself. As Dr. LePera says, "You were never broken, just coping."

Numbers 13 reveals the power of how we think about ourselves. This is the story of the 12 spies checking out the Promised Land the Israelites would soon live in. In fact, in Numbers 13:2, we read that God told Moses to send the men in to explore the land of Canaan, "which I am giving to the Israelites." However, *I am giving* is written in the past tense. This promise of the land was given over 170 times before the Israelites possessed it. You would assume this story would progress differently.

But if you know the story, the spies saw the people who lived there and became afraid. 10 of the 12 spies spread a bad report and convinced the tribes to live in fear. The craziest verse in all of this story happens in verse 33. Notice the language. After they spread the bad report, they said, "We seemed like grasshoppers in our own eyes, and we looked the same to them." Metaphorically speaking, were they grasshoppers? No. Did they create a false narrative because of how they viewed themselves? Yes. In other words, how we think determines how we live. If we view ourselves like grasshoppers, that's what we'll be.

Did you know grasshoppers do not have ears? They "hear" through vibrations. Remember that verse in Romans 10:17 that says, "Faith comes from hearing?" When we don't listen to the right voices, we shrink ourselves into insignificance. That, my friends, is not how the Creator of the Universe views you.

Let the words of Don Keathley, teacher at the Digital Cathedral and founder of Global Grace Seminary, remind you of your original design, "All sin is mistaken identity. Adam sinned when he forgot who he was. Most of us sin because we either forgot who we were or never knew who we were. Jesus came to take away the false identity **in our minds**. The Gospel is not a story of separation by sin, the Gospel is a story of a Father who is so faithful to us and loved us so much that he came in human form to reveal to us and demonstrate for us in Jesus what our original design actually looked like."

You are not a grasshopper. You are not broken.

Wholeness is your truth. Pseudoscientist Dr. Masaru Emoto talks about the power of words – he labeled Petri dishes of water with positive and negative words and emotions. Some labeled 'love' and others labeled 'hate'. Dr. Emoto proved that when water was labeled with positive intentions and then frozen, the water droplets formed perfect hexagonal shapes and sacred geometry. The frozen water that was labeled negatively would be blurry and unsymmetrical. If our thoughts and emotions can change the molecular structure of water, think about the reality that our bodies are 50% - 70% water. Your voice matters. You are significant. You are whole. You are amazing, and it's time you start noticing why.

Today's Work

1. How does what you read today help conquer your negative thought from Day 1?

2. Repeat your personal motto.

3. Guided Meditation – Take a moment and meditate on the following statement from W. Paul Young, author of *The Shack*. Be free from all distractions. Be still. After reading, either close your eyes and soak it in or keep repeating what he said. Then, I want you to write or draw what you hear, see, sense, or feel from the Spirit.

"Wholeness is when the ways of your being are an expression of the truth of your being. Pause and take a deep breath. The Father, the Son, and the Holy Spirit are especially fond of you. You are the melody being sung inside three-part harmony."

Bonus – sometime today, listen to *2 Pastors And A Mic* podcast episode 29 titled, *"You're Not Broken."*

Scan the QR Code below for more information or visit saintsnotsinners.com and click on the 21 Day Devo tab for more information.

4. Today's challenge – How can you take today's devotional and encourage someone else with it?

day three

. . .

Loved

WHAT IF I told you you're loved simply because you exist?

Have you ever noticed that when Jesus does most of His miracles, we are rarely given people's names? In the first chapter of Mark alone, we see Jesus heal a demon-possessed man, a man with leprosy, and Peter's sick mother-in-law. (Some scholars believe the reason Peter denied Jesus three times is because Jesus healed his mother-in-law…I'm kidding). Instead of knowing their names, we're often only given their gender and condition – the man with the withered hand, the woman with the blood issue, the blind man, etc. This is even common in our own culture today. We tend to label people by their gender and conditions – 'he's divorced, she's had an abortion, he's an alcoholic, she's a user, he's battling depression, she sleeps around.' We love to label people by their struggles and mistakes because it's easier to look down on others for doing things we wouldn't.

However, in Christ, you don't have to be identified by your issues. It doesn't matter what people call you; it only matters what you respond to. People may know your history, but don't let that affect your destiny. Your true label as a son or daughter of God is one simple word – LOVED.

It's cliche only because we roll our eyes as we think we've heard it before. Yet, if we were to be honest about how we think God views us, it usually lines up more with the vivid picture of a middle school boy plucking flower petals to see if his crush likes him – 'She loves me, she loves me not.' We believe God loves us when we're good and then frowns upon us when we're bad. That cycle is exhausting. **It's impossible to follow God when you are unsure about how He feels towards you.** You will never be able to love well until you recognize how loved you are by your Father in Heaven.

Brennan Manning, a man who preached the grace of God until he passed away several years ago, believes the Lord Jesus is going to ask us one question and only one question when we see our Maker face to face. He believes God will look at us and ask, "Did you really believe that I loved you? That I desired you? That I waited for you day after day? That I longed to hear the sound of your voice?" He goes on to preach that many of us who are so faithful in ministry and church attendance will reply to that question with a heartbreaking 'no.' They'll say they heard incredible sermons and teachings and even believed it occasionally through life, but they really just thought it was the Christian way of patting people on the back and cheering them on. And that is the difference between real believers and the many people who say they follow Jesus in our churches today.

Bottom line – Jesus is our hero. Not because He comes and destroys our enemies but because He shed His blood on the cross for our enemies. He's the One who has rescued us from sin and death. He is our lover and friend, ascribing to us unsurpassable worth. The cross is not the symbol of Christianity; the empty tomb is! Jesus is alive, and

He's freeing us from the religious grave clothes that keep us in bondage. Break free from rituals and rules and run into the loving embrace of the Father – because *we are His beloved!* As author Jack Frost says, "Moving from slavery to sonship or daughterhood is a matter of reaching the place where you get up in the morning feeling so loved and accepted in your Father's heart that your whole purpose for existence becomes looking for ways to give that love away to the next person you meet." So, remember you're loved, and there's nothing you can do about it!

Today's Work

1. How does what you read today help conquer your negative thought from Day 1?

2. Repeat your personal motto.

3. Guided Meditation – Go listen to the song "Pieces" by Bethel Music. Be free from all distractions. Be still. Either close your eyes and listen or read along with the lyrics. Which lyrics stood out the most and why? Write or draw what you hear, see, sense, or feel from the Spirit.

Scan the QR Code below for more information or visit saintsnotsinners.com and click on the 21 Day Devo tab for more information.

4. Today's challenge – How can you take today's devotional and encourage someone else with it?

day four

. . .

Unique

WHAT IF I told you you're God's favorite, and it's time you start living like it?

Today, I want to enlighten your individuality! I'm going to explain how *God does not love us equally*. 'But haven't you been trying to tell us that He loves us all unconditionally?' Yes, He does! But that doesn't mean He loves us equally. 'So, you're saying He loves certain people more than others?' No, I'm not saying that, and no, God doesn't love certain people more than others.

God doesn't love us equally; He loves us uniquely! Here's what I mean – if God loved us all equally, then we'd be replaceable. Think about it this way. I have three kids, and I say I love my kids the same, but that is not true. I say I love my kids equally, but that is not true. It doesn't mean I love one more than the other. It means I love them all differently because they all are unique and irreplaceable. If one of my kids passed, I couldn't just make another one to replace them. That thought alone is asinine. Why? Because they were created by an incredibly passionate Designer with a purpose in mind. They are, in fact, irreplaceable. You are irreplaceable! God made only one of you! You were created on purpose for a purpose, and there is no one in the world quite like you. No one else can do what you are called to do. No one else has your platform, personality, and people to influence. You are the perfect person God created to do what He wants to do in and through you. Because you are irreplaceable, you have an incredible responsibility to be uniquely you.

So, stop trying to be someone else because 'God can't bless the person you pretend to be.' He wants to bless you! He wants to love you in your own unique ways. He wants you to celebrate your individuality, personality, strengths, and weaknesses. He wants you to live life to the fullest, knowing that there is no one like you on Earth.

What does God's face look like when He thinks about you? If the image of God's face has anything but a smile, you have misunderstood the reality of His unconditional love for you. Because our human relationships are broken, we tend to project earthly relationships onto God. We refuse to believe that God is really as loving as He says He is, so we create a god in our own image. We want God to be as gloomy, pessimistic, fussy, rude, legalistic, narrow-minded, judgmental, violent, unforgiving, and unloving as we are. We end up basing our identity on how well we are doing spiritually rather than on what God has declared over us in Christ. We must relate to God in light of who He really is, not just who we think or hope Him to be.

Today's Work

1. How does what you read today help conquer your negative thought from Day 1?

2. Repeat your personal motto.

3. Guided Meditation – Scan the QR Code below and watch today's quick teaching. Or visit saintsnotsinners.com and click on the 21 Day Devo tab for more information. After watching the video, I want you to close your eyes and focus on His facial features and expressions. As you process, come back to this page and write or draw what God's face looks like when He thinks about you.

4. Today's challenge – How can you take today's devotional and encourage someone else with it?

day five

. . .

Chosen

W<small>HAT IF</small> I told you you're wanted more than you could even imagine?

Have you ever been rejected? In my opinion, not feeling wanted is one of the worst kinds of feelings we can experience. Many of us can think of a relationship that didn't work out the way we had hoped it to. And yet, even as you read this, flashbacks or current realities might cause your stomach to churn and depression to set in. It might not seem significant in your season of loneliness, but the comforting reality of Jesus is that we're wanted, pursued, and chosen! God desires us more than we may know.

My goal is to help build up your confidence in believing you matter... to believe that you are wanted... to believe that you are predestined for greatness!

God chose you from the beginning of time (Ephesians 1:4-5). He predestined all of us to be conformed to His image. However, we need to address the issue of predestination that a lot of well-meaning Christians misunderstand. The word 'predestined' is used only four times throughout Scripture (twice in Romans and twice in Ephesians). Understanding the context of these passages will help you understand what predestination means. Romans and Ephesians are books written to Gentiles. Why is that important? Because this thought was controversial at the time. What Paul was trying to communicate is that it was always a part of God's plan to include Gentiles into the family of God! (Notice how you won't find the word predestination in any books written to Jews: Hebrews, James, 1+2 Peter, 1+2+3 John). Predestination is about God's choice to predestine all people (Jew and Gentile, male and female, etc.) for sonship through Jesus. It's our choice to remain as an orphan or live as a child in the Royal family! It has nothing to do with God predestining people for a certain afterlife experience. It has everything to do with you understanding your greatness now. Because a great God lives in you, He has empowered you to do incredible things today!

Start by speaking confidence into your soul! You are unique, and God created you to be you. God gave you the influence to love the people around you well. God gave you purpose, and when He thinks about you, His smile can't be contained. You are His beloved, and He is proud of you! Don't be consumed with trying to change THE world… be consumed with trying to change YOUR world today!

Today's Work

1. How does what you read today help conquer your negative thought from Day 1?

2. Repeat your personal motto.

3. Guided Meditation – Go listen to the song "Who You Say I Am" by Hillsong. Be free from all distractions. Be still. Either close your eyes and listen or read along with the lyrics. Which lyrics stood out the most and why? Write or draw what you hear, see, sense, or feel from the Spirit.

Scan the QR Code below for more information or visit saintsnotsinners.com and click on the 21 Day Devo tab for more information.

4. Today's challenge – How can you take today's devotional and encourage someone else with it?

day six

· · ·

Qualified

WHAT IF I told you you're seated at the King's table, and He's delighted by your presence?

The Kentucky Derby has put my hometown on the map. Every single year, I know nothing about the horses who qualify for the race, but you better believe I still bet on my favorite name. To no surprise, I have never won my bets. Every year, there is always some type of unforeseen drama, but no one could have predicted what happened in 2019. We saw the first disqualification in the history of the event. It took 145 derby races to see a horse get disqualified for breaking the rules, and people went bananas. Over 9 million dollars was lost in the sports betting world, and it was the talk of the town. However, if you ask someone who actually watches horse racing regularly, they'd inform you this disqualification happens all the time in weekly horse races all across our country. It just never occurred during the event dubbed "The most exciting two minutes in sports."

Did the jockey and horse make a mistake? Yup

Did they reap the consequence of that mistake? Yup

Does it suck? If you care...

The tie-in? The beautiful thing about the Kingdom of God is that even your mistakes don't disqualify you from His love and anointing.

Cheesy? Maybe

But the truth remains. You can't disqualify yourself from sitting at the table with the King. You might have made some poor choices, but your mistakes don't define you. You might have to suffer the natural consequences of your decisions, but God's anointing and power have never left your life. You are qualified, anointed, empowered, and equipped to continue to expand the love of Jesus wherever you are. So, lift your head, focus on Jesus, remember your position as a child of God, and continue to run your race!

Today's Work

1. How does what you read today help conquer your negative thought from Day 1?

2. Repeat your personal motto.

3. Guided Meditation – Scan the QR Code below and watch today's video. Or visit saintsnotsinners.com and click on the 21 Day Devo tab for more information. What stood out as you watched? After watching

the video, I want you to close your eyes and ask the Spirit to give you three words/phrases to affirm your significance. Because you are good enough. You are qualified.

4. Today's challenge – How can you take today's devotional and encourage someone else with it?

day seven

. . .

Worthy

WHAT IF I told you your worth is determined by God, not by your accomplishments?

When we don't feel worthy, we become clingers for security, status, and stuff. We begin to believe our religious performances are what gives us our worth. When we do this, we ignore the gift of grace and subject our well-being with the works of the law.

Philippians 1:27 is often quoted as a rebuttal because it says, "Whatever happens, conduct yourselves in a manner worthy of the gospel of Christ." However, to live worthy does not mean to live deserving. It means to have the right response to the Gospel. Believing in Jesus does not make you worthy. Believing in Jesus simply activates the truth that you've always been worthy. Worthiness is knowing you're His.

Our performance does not dictate our worth in the Kingdom of God, but it does dictate how much of the Kingdom of God flows through you today. Your life choices don't make you worthy. Worthiness is a gift that empowers your life choices.

We are made worthy by faith. But have you ever asked whose faith makes you and I worthy? Is it based on my faith? And how do you get more faith? How do you just trust? Because I'M TRYING! Let me blow your mind because I am done feeling bad for not having great faith.

Faith is a person, and His name is Jesus. He is faith personified. Jesus is your life, and He has great faith for you and in you. Did you know sometimes well-meaning translators mistranslate verses in the Bible? When it happens, it can create a lot of confusion. For example, look up these verses in the original Greek to see the mistranslation for yourself.

- Romans 3:22 says, "Righteousness is given through faith IN Jesus..." However, it should read, "Righteousness is given through faith FROM Jesus..."
- Galatians 2:20 says, "I have been crucified with Christ and I no longer live, but Christ lives in me. The life I now live in the body, I live by faith IN the Son of God, who loved me and gave himself for me." However, it should read, "I live by faith FROM the Son of God..."
- Galatians 3:22 says, "But Scripture has locked up everything under the control of sin, so that what was promised, being given through faith IN Jesus Christ, might be given to those who believe." However, that last sentence should read, "being given through faith FROM Jesus..."

You don't need more faith; you need to rest in His because His faith is the basis of your faith. As 2 Timothy 2:13 reveals, "If we are faithless, He remains faithful." Thank God! Faith is not a work; it's the joyful acceptance of what Jesus has done. What if your faith can only grow when you recognize it's not yours to grow; it's simply yours to grasp?

Today's Work

1. How does what you read today help conquer your negative thought from Day 1?

2. Repeat your personal motto.

3. Guided Meditation – Go listen to the song "Fountain (I am good)" by Mosaic MSC. Be free from all distractions. Be still. Either close your eyes and listen or read along with the lyrics. Which lyrics stood out the most and why? Write or draw what you hear, see, sense, or feel from the Spirit.

   Bonus – sometime today, listen to 2 Pastors And A Mic podcast episode 107 titled, "New Year, New You – Faith."

   Scan the QR Code below for more information or visit saintsnotsinners.com and click on the 21 Day Devo tab for more information.

4. Today's challenge – How can you take today's devotional and encourage someone else with it?

day eight

· · ·

Secured

WHAT IF I told you your soul is safe and secured in Christ, even when religion tells you otherwise?

When we don't feel secure, we become pleasers. We start exhausting ourselves with good Christian performances while trying to please a God who is already pleased with us.

Yesterday, we talked about not needing more faith but rather resting in the faith Jesus has in us. We are made worthy by faith; it's just not our faith that makes us worthy. People get scared with messages like this because they think people will just abandon their faith. Or say – 'oh well, I guess I don't need faith because it's not even mine.' But as someone who has literally experienced this revelation, it actually does the opposite. My faith is strengthened when I rest in His.

We looked at three Scriptures yesterday, but I purposefully left off the rebuttal from Hebrews 11:6, which says, "Without faith, it is impossible to please God." SEE!! Yes, it's true. But if we believe faith means having the right ideas and right beliefs without ever doubting them, then maybe we've misunderstood faith and doubt. What this passage means is without faith in Jesus, it is impossible to AGREE with God. So, people keep working to try to please God by faith without realizing God is already pleased with them. Without faith, you cannot bear fruit. Yes, it takes faith to embrace the Kingdom of God and put others first. It takes faith to love like Jesus. But Jesus didn't say they will know you are my disciples by your faith, knowledge of Scripture, or your ability to believe the right things. He said you will know you are my disciples by your love (John 13:35).

My friend, rest in the security the Father provides. You belong even if you don't know exactly what you believe. The Gospel does not demand your faith; it supplies it. The Gospel is not an invitation to accept Jesus; it's a declaration that the Father has already accepted you. His faith is what provides security. So be confident in His faith and watch your individual faith grow as you grasp His.

Today's Work

1. How does what you read today help conquer your negative thought from Day 1?

2. Repeat your personal motto.

3. Guided Meditation – Go listen to the song "Remember" by Bryan & Katie Torwalt. Be free from all distractions. Be still. Either close your eyes and listen or read along with the lyrics. Which lyrics stood out the most and why? Write or draw what you hear, see, sense, or feel from the Spirit.

Scan the QR Code below for more information or visit saintsnotsinners.com and click on the 21 Day Devo tab for more information.

4. Today's challenge – How can you take today's devotional and encourage someone else with it?

day nine

· · ·

Accepted

WHAT IF I told you you're accepted, and it's time to stop trying out for a position you already have?

When we don't feel accepted, we become conformers. We try to earn a spot by fitting in instead of standing out. We see this even with King Saul when he told the prophet Samuel in 1 Samuel 15:24, "I have sinned. I violated the Lord's command and your instructions. I was afraid of the men and so I gave in to them." Peer pressure is real, but it reveals a lie we believe internally.

One of the most famous stories in the Bible is the parable of the prodigal son found in Luke 15. After the son had left his father's house, blown his inheritance on wild living, and hit rock bottom, he decided to return home. He didn't decide to come home because of his love for his dad, even though he has his apology letter memorized. He comes home because he's starving and alone. He has no more money, food, or shelter. His motivation is survival. How does his father respond when he sees his son coming home?

If you know the story, there are so many incredible revelations connected with what happens next. The father ignores the speech and embraces his son. The son thought he was no longer worthy of that title. He was going to ask his dad to make him like one of his hired servants. But notice what the father puts on his son in verse 22 – a robe, a ring, and sandals. The robe speaks to forgiveness and righteousness (love and grace cover sin and shame). The ring speaks to royalty (value and belonging). The sandals speak to identity because SERVANTS DON'T WEAR SANDALS; SONS DO (sonship).

Jesus was challenging His audience's mentality. The same is true today - we must turn the orphan mindset into royal authority. Our DNA is changed. We are accepted. Can you accept your acceptance?

It's time to quit trying out for a position that Christ has already given you. Quit trying to earn a spot when God has already accepted you as you are. Do not talk yourself out of the position God has for you. Your position never changes. Servants don't wear sandals.

For the record, could you imagine what would have happened if the younger son encountered his older, religious brother before he experienced the embrace and acceptance of his father? How we represent the Father matters in this adventure we call life.

Today's Work

1. How does what you read today help conquer your negative thought from Day 1?

2. Repeat your personal motto.

3. Guided Meditation – Scan the QR Code below and watch today's video. Or visit saintsnotsinners.com and click on the 21 Day Devo tab for more information. We're going to practice self-love. After you participate in today's meditation, come back to this page and write or draw what you hear, see, sense, or feel from the Spirit.

4. Today's challenge – How can you take today's devotional and encourage someone else with it?

day ten

· · ·

Valued

WHAT IF I told you your behavior doesn't have the power to change God's mind about you?

When we don't feel valued, we become performers. Martha falls for this lie in Luke 10 when she's busy with all the work it takes to entertain guests. She informs Jesus it's His responsibility to reprimand her sister, Mary, and make her help. I love what Jesus tells Martha, "You are worried and upset about many things, but few things are needed – or indeed only one. Mary has chosen what is better, and it will not be taken away from her." In other words, we try to please God by our performance without realizing we're already pleasing to Him by just being.

One of the greatest lies we could ever entertain is believing we're not good enough. Do you really know how valuable you are? Jesus reminds us through a parable in Luke 12:7 when He says, "The very hairs of your head are all numbered. Don't be afraid; you are more valuable than sparrows." Have you ever really sat with that verse before? Do you really know your value?

You cannot disappoint God. Disappointment revolves around unmet expectations and imagination. I don't know if you have ever critically thought about it before, but if God is all-knowing (omniscient), you can never disappoint God because He has no expectation of you. If God had expectations of you, that would mean He didn't know something because the only way to be disappointed is to have expectations. As the author of *The Shack*, W. Paul Young, says, "God grieves for and with you when you act inside your lies and darkness. But not because God expected more from you. He grieves the identity we often refuse to believe. It is in the gap of lies we believe about ourselves that we project onto God (disappointment and abandonment)."

Think about the power of these statements:

- You belong to me, and I belong to you.
- The universe is better because you are in it.
- I love you.
- I am especially fond of you.

These statements are how God speaks over you. Remember, God knows you completely and fully. You don't surprise God. God delights in you. Your performance does not dictate God's affection towards you. You do not have the power to change God's mind about you. You are enough.

Today's Work

1. How does what you read today help conquer your negative thought from Day 1?

2. Repeat your personal motto.

3. Guided Meditation – Take a minute to contemplate the four statements from today's devotional. As you process each one, write or draw what you hear, see, sense, or feel from the Spirit.

4. Today's challenge – How can you take today's devotional and encourage someone else with it?

day eleven

• • •

Royal

WHAT IF I told you you're already walking in the inheritance?

Once you know your worth, security, acceptance, and value, your position as royalty is easier to embrace. Remember that one time some dude claimed to be the King of the Jews and then was brutally murdered by a bunch of religious, seminary-educated, church-going, and bloodthirsty zealots? And because that event happened in our past, we don't need to wait until Easter to celebrate our current, permanent reality. You don't have to get right before you walk into a church service this weekend. What Christ did 2,000 years ago already made you right. Therefore, you can walk into any church service this weekend with confidence and your head held high to celebrate who Christ is. Why? Because you're already a part of the royal family. You may just need to awaken to your royal reality.

How are we royal? 1 Peter 2:9 claims we're a royal priesthood. Do you understand what that means? Not only are we royalty, but we're a part of the priesthood! In 70 A.D., the Temple in Jerusalem was completely destroyed. The destruction fulfilled many prophecies, but one of the most significant things that occurred was the complete destruction of the Levitical line of priests. Why is this important? Because God never wanted to have one man be the only person to represent the relationship God had with mankind. What Jesus did brings direct relationship to every human! No more priests needed to intercede on your behalf. You are a priest, and you have direct access to the Father.

As a priest, you're also a part of the royal family. How so? In Revelation 3:21, Jesus says, "To the one who is victorious, I will give the right to sit with me on my throne, just as I was victorious and sat down with my Father on his throne." In other Scriptures, they mention that Jesus sits at the "right hand of God." This doesn't mean Jesus sits on a different throne next to God. It means He's seated with God. In other words, on Abba's lap! So where are we? We're seated with Jesus on Abba's lap. You're sitting on the throne, not as God but with God.

Have you ever thought about the fact that you're currently walking in your spiritual inheritance? If you're not aware, someone has to die before you gain an inheritance... well Jesus died, and He left us an inheritance – that is proper Kingdom living that's full of hope, life, love, and peace. An inheritance of royal priesthood. An inheritance by promise, not by performance. He's crowned us not just with righteousness but with the responsibility to love people well and participate in the Kingdom of God here on Earth. To live as if the good news of Jesus is actually good news.

Regardless of what any preacher may say or how you feel about your own performance, you belong because Jesus already crowned you... forever.

Today's Work

1. How does what you read today help conquer your negative thought from Day 1?

2. Repeat your personal motto.

3. Guided Meditation – Scan the QR Code below and watch today's video. Or visit saintsnotsinners.com and click on the 21 Day Devo tab for more information. After watching the video, I want you to come back to this page and write or draw your experience in the white room. What did you hear, see, sense, or feel from the Spirit?

4. Today's challenge – How can you take today's devotional and encourage someone else with it?

day twelve

. . .

Forgiven

WHAT IF I told you you're forgiven even if you don't confess?

Isn't it ironic how Christians tend to argue against something they actually say to entice non-believers to be a part of their 'church'? We tell people they are already forgiven by God; they just need to believe it. Then, we refuse to believe it about ourselves because we still sin. Thank God our identity is not performance-based but positionally sound in Christ. You're forgiven, no ifs, ands, or buts. Still don't believe me? If you didn't physically exist during the brutal murder of Jesus, yet He forgave the world of their sin, how many of your sins were actually forgiven? That's right... ALL. That means all of your sins – past, present, and future – all are forgiven. That even means the sins you forget to 'confess' are all forgiven. Isn't it crazy to believe the Gospel is actually GOOD NEWS?!?!

I'll take it a step further. Forgiveness has always been God's gift to humanity. As Paul said, "God reconciled the world to Himself through Jesus." But now, we're not just forgiven; we're justified. Justified means 'just as if we've never sinned.' What Jesus did on the cross actually makes us innocent, never guilty, permanently forgiven. How can I say that? Those aren't my words; those are the words of several different authors of Scripture who write that God takes away the sin of the world (John 1:29), remembers our sin no more by nailing it to the cross (Colossians 2:14, Hebrews 8:12, Hebrews 10:17-18), that God has removed our transgressions as far as the east is to the west (Psalm 103:12), and even Isaiah prophesied this would happen through the Messiah (Isaiah 43:25). In Christ there is no more condemnation (John 3:18, Romans 8:1). If God does not remember our sins, why do we? The more we focus on our sins, the more of a problem sin is. This is why many can never overcome their 'issues' because they're focusing more on their behavior than their Savior. We must let go of our past and cast our own sin away from our memory because Christ already has.

Some believe the only way God could bring you into perfect union with Him is if He refuses to allow sin to be put in your account. So, if you believe sin makes you unclean, imperfect, impure, and unholy... but it's not in your account... you might be more clean, perfect, pure, and holy than you think. Then the religious person responds – 'but won't that create pride?!' Impossible because you didn't clean yourself up. Jesus did on your behalf. Usually, in anger, the next religious response is – 'but won't people willingly keep on sinning if they know they're permanently forgiven?!' Impossible, because knowing you're forgiven actually empowers you to destroy whatever illusion of sin you think separates you from God.

Everything you think you want in sin actually gets fulfilled in Christ, AND THEN SOME. It produces actual joy, peace, and love. The people who abuse forgiveness don't live with joy, peace, and love. I believe there is nothing that satisfies our soul more than resting securely in the presence of God, knowing we're completely forgiven.

Grace does not give us freedom to sin; it empowers us to live free with Jesus. As Pastor Bill Vanderbush says, "Grace disempowers sins ability to manipulate God out of loving you. Grace does not have the power to tell God whether or not He can love and accept you. That would make the power of sin greater than the power of righteousness. It's not your ability to keep law and rules that demonstrates your character. It's your ability to manage freedom. What you choose to do when you're free to do anything is what reveals the condition of your heart." No one can claim forgiveness apart from Christ, yet in Christ, we're made complete, holy, without blemish, and free from accusation because it's not based on our efforts; it's based on His! And that's the good news! We're forgiven, and there is nothing we can do about it.

Today's Work

1. How does what you read today help conquer your negative thought from Day 1?

2. Repeat your personal motto.

3. Guided Meditation – Go listen to the song "Mercy" by Bethel Music. Be free from all distractions. Be still. Either close your eyes and listen or read along with the lyrics. Which lyrics stood out the most and why? Write or draw what you hear, see, sense, or feel from the Spirit.

   Scan the QR Code below for more information or visit saintsnotsinners.com and click on the 21 Day Devo tab for more information.

4. Today's challenge – How can you take today's devotional and encourage someone else with it?

day thirteen

. . .

Blameless

WHAT IF I told you you're more innocent than you think you are?

One false emotion all of humanity deals with is guilt. We all feel guilt over things we shouldn't have said or done or things we should have said or done. I recently asked people what they feel guilty for, and the responses were very similar. Responses such as time with family/kids/God, parenting or lack thereof, anger, communication, life decisions and regrets, addictions, where money is spent and the lack of generosity, self-care/rest/me time, etc.

Guilt is a real emotion we all feel, but it is a liar and a thief and has been robbing some of us of the best moments of our lives. Good news, there is no such thing as guilt in the Kingdom of God, and I'll prove it. In John 20, the first message Jesus told his disciples to preach after the cross was to proclaim the permanent reality of a forgiven state of being for all people. The only reason people feel guilty is that the Church hasn't done a good job telling the world they're forgiven. All of humanity has been right with God for 2,000 years, but if you don't believe it, it won't matter or manifest. The reason why we must believe we are forgiven is not to make it true (it's always been true); rather, it's to make it true to you personally.

Remember, if your sins have been forgiven and forgotten by God, why are you holding on to them? We talked through some of those verses yesterday. Let's look at two of them in greater detail and marinate in the truth...

- Colossians 2:13-15 "When you were dead in your sins and in the uncircumcision of your flesh, God made you alive with Christ. He forgave us all our sins, having canceled the charge of our legal indebtedness, which stood against us and condemned us; he has taken it away, nailing it to the cross. And having disarmed the powers and authorities, he made a public spectacle of them, triumphing over them by the cross."

When did God make you alive with Christ? When did He forgive sins? When you believed? When you confessed? Or did He take it away and actually nail it to the cross? Did He actually disarm the powers and authorities – triumphing over them by the cross?

- Hebrews 10:15-18 "The Holy Spirit also testifies to us about this. First he says: "This is the covenant I will make with them after that time, says the Lord. I will put my laws in their hearts, and I will write them on their minds." Then he adds: "Their sins and lawless acts I will remember no more." And where these have been forgiven, sacrifice for sin is no longer necessary."

So, did God lie about remembering sins or not? And when did this state of forgiveness occur? Was Jesus's sacrifice once and for all or not?

Once we critically look at the truth, it reveals a permanent identity that creates genuine confidence. If there is no more condemnation because of Christ (Romans 8:1), why are you condemning yourself? If there's no guilt found at the Father's table, why are you sitting at the table with a plate full of guilt?

Now, some will say that guilt is a good thing. That guilt led someone to make something right. I've even heard a pastor once say, "Guilt is like a broken bone, letting you know something needs to be fixed." Although I understand the thought process, it's still not a right thought. Why? Because God never uses guilt to motivate you to do something right. The motivation always stems from love. You seek reconciliation not because you feel guilty but because you love.

In order to live confidently, you must let go of your guilt. You are blameless, and there is nothing you can do about it.

Today's Work

1. How does what you read today help conquer your negative thought from Day 1?

2. Repeat your personal motto.

3. Guided Meditation – Go listen to the song "Blameless" by Dara Maclean. Be free from all distractions. Be still. Either close your eyes

and listen or read along with the lyrics. Which lyrics stood out the most and why? Write or draw what you hear, see, sense, or feel from the Spirit.

Scan the QR Code below for more information or visit saintsnotsinners.com and click on the 21 Day Devo tab for more information.

4. Today's challenge – How can you take today's devotional and encourage someone else with it?

day fourteen

. . .

Righteous

WHAT IF I told you your righteousness is not tied to your righteous acts?

I hear the phrase 'you ain't right' on a regular basis. I'm easily influenced to do or say something outrageous just for the laughs. Although my behavior isn't 'right' sometimes, it doesn't define my permanent 'right' standing as a son in the Kingdom of God. That's right, all of us are already standing 'right' before God as forgiven, blameless, and clean because of Jesus.

What you're about to read may be shocking to you. Not because you'll disagree but because it may require you to rewire the way you think. Can the Gospel message really be this simple?

Righteousness is not something you get when you stop sinning. Righteousness is not given or taken from us based on our performance. Righteousness is already ours based on the performance of Jesus.

However, righteousness means nothing for us today unless we own it. If God is righteous and He lives in me, I'm righteous in Christ. If God is complete and He lives in me, I'm complete in Christ. If God is perfect and He lives in me, I'm perfect in Christ. Romans 10:4 says, "Christ is the culmination of the law so that there may be righteousness for everyone who believes." Belief is important but belief doesn't make it true. It's always been true; belief simply activates what has always been true. **Because I am in Christ, God sees me according to how Jesus has lived, not by how I act.**

Let this reality sink in. In Christ, God no longer sees me as a sinner saved by grace; He now sees me as a saint saved by grace. Regardless of my situation, He sees Jesus in me; He sees the righteousness of Christ. The life Jesus lived on Earth has now been credited in full to us.

The biggest hindrance to receiving this incredible truth is many of us are more comfortable being slaves than being free. Why? We like having something to measure ourselves by and strive for. It allows us to control how God distributes His love and grace. It makes sense to believe we're blessed because we follow the 'rules.' And isn't it so humble to think of ourselves as such wretched, dirty sinners? However, none of these things are actually Jesus-focused. Stop striving for something you already have. Stop following rules and start following Jesus. When you live to receive blessings, you miss the revelation that you're already blessed.

By the way, it's not humble to think lowly of yourself. That's false humility and a slap to the face of your Creator. Proper humility isn't thinking less of yourself but rather thinking of yourself less. You are a son or daughter of the living King. You are royalty (1 Peter 2:9)! You are His masterpiece (Ephesians 2:10)! It's time you start living like it.

We stand 'right' because we're standing on the finished work of Jesus. We say things like, 'yeah, but we still sin.' Well, remember, forgiveness is based on Jesus. We need to stop focusing so much on our sin because it's already been dealt with. We're not to live sin conscious; we're to live Savior conscious. We don't have a sin issue; we have a belief issue. Jesus doesn't want your sins; **He wants you!** Righteousness isn't what you do; it's determined by who you believe, and who you believe will determine how you behave. When you start thinking differently, you start living differently. Paul reiterated this in Galatians 2:21, "I do not set aside the grace of God, for if righteousness could be gained through the law, Christ died for nothing." So be confident in your right standing before God. You are as righteous as you'll ever be, and there's nothing you can do about it.

Today's Work

1. How does what you read today help conquer your negative thought from Day 1?

2. Repeat your personal motto.

3. Guided Meditation – Scan the QR Code below and watch today's fun yet shocking video. Or visit saintsnotsinners.com and click on the 21 Day Devo tab for more information. In the video, you'll be instructed to do something today. Once you have completed the task, come back to this page and write or draw your experience. What did you hear, see, sense, or feel from the Spirit?

4. Today's challenge – How can you take today's devotional and encourage someone else with it?

day fifteen

. . .

Known

WHAT IF I told you God has never crossed His arms at you?

We want to be known but are often scared of the shame that might come from being known. Researcher and author Brené Brown says, "We cultivate love when we allow our most vulnerable and powerful selves to be deeply seen and known." In order to do this, we must be honest with ourselves and find safe people to process this with. Faith in Jesus is not about a one-time decision; rather, it's a discovery of how known and loved we are.

Have you ever contemplated how David is known most for his affair with Bathsheba, and yet the Bible declares twice that he is a man after God's own heart? (1 Samuel 13:14, Acts 13:22). Maybe it's more important to listen to the labels God gives us instead of how we often define ourselves. Maybe it's time to start resting in our identity instead of striving for one.

Here's what I mean – it's time to stop hungering and thirsting for more of Jesus. I know it sounds wrong to read, but hear me out. I was taught to constantly hunger and thirst for more of God. I never looked at the teaching critically because it sounded good. However, it's actually the opposite of what following Jesus is about. Think about it this way – to hunger and thirst is to lack something. Hunger and thirst are terms used by orphans. When you're even taught to hunger and thirst for more knowledge and revelation, you'll never be satisfied with 'love like Jesus' ... which is the entirety of the Gospel. We oftentimes would rather bury ourselves in the Scriptures, prayer closets, or at a table of 'theologians' debating theology instead of going out of our way to love people...all people.

You might be thinking, BUT Jesus said blessed are those who hunger and thirst for righteousness (Matthew 5:6). Indeed, however, Jesus was talking to Jews under the old covenant law. He also concluded that verse by saying, 'AND THEY WILL BE FILLED...'

Fast forward to John 6. Jesus is teaching on how He is the bread of life. He says in verse 35, "Whoever comes to me will never go hungry, and whoever believes in me will never be thirsty." Once you know your righteousness isn't tied to your behavior but found in the person of Jesus... you understand you're filled... permanently. Filled with purpose, belonging, acceptance, and value. Filled to fill others.

You can't be righteous by what you do. You can't be favored or blessed because you give, fast, and pray. You can't be anointed because of your study. You already are righteous, favored, blessed, and anointed because of Jesus in you! The only thing you think you lack is made up in the way you think. This is why David is a man after God's own heart, and so are you! You are already completely known by the Creator, and He is proud of you.

Have you ever noticed the crowds that followed Jesus and how often Jesus needed to retreat from them? Why is that? Maybe it's because it's exhausting having to spiritually fill people who think they lack what He already provides. The crowds hungered and thirsted for what Jesus did. Therefore, they were never satisfied in who He was... resulting in never being satisfied in who they were. Today, we are often motivated to follow Jesus for what He does rather than for who He is.

It's time to stop longing for more of whatever you think you lack. The only longing you should desire is how you can give away what already belongs to you. Theologian and author of the Mirror Bible Translation, Francois Du Toit, says it this way, "We are designed to participate in our divine origin simply by reflecting, not striving." You lack nothing (not my words, but David's in Psalm 23). Hungering and thirsting for more isn't the Gospel. It's not even good Christian behavior. It's actually anti-gospel as you refuse to believe Christ is sufficient.

I'm not saying you shouldn't read the Scriptures, pray in a closet, or discuss theology with others. You should definitely do those things. I am saying, however, those things don't gain you whatever it is you think you lack. You're already seated at the King's table, and He is thrilled to be in your presence! He knows you, so let's stop living like orphans and recognize our place in the Royal Family.

Today's Work

1. How does what you read today help conquer your negative thought from Day 1?

2. Repeat your personal motto.

3. Guided Meditation – Go listen to the song "Where I Belong (Father's Heart)" by Hill City Worship. Be free from all distractions. Be still. Either close your eyes and listen or read along with the lyrics. Which lyrics stood out the most and why? Write or draw what you hear, see, sense, or feel from the Spirit.

Scan the QR Code below for more information or visit saintsnotsinners.com and click on the 21 Day Devo tab for more information.

4. Today's challenge – How can you take today's devotional and encourage someone else with it?

day sixteen

· · ·

Perfect

WHAT IF I told you your behavior doesn't dictate your perfection?

Have you ever thought about how many prostitutes are recorded in the Bible? Rahab, Lilith, Gomer, Dinah (Jacob's daughter), Tamar (daughter-in-law of Judah), the Moabite women, the Midianite harlot, Jephthah's mother, Oholah and Oholibah (Ezekiel 23), two mothers in 1 Kings 3, the woman with the alabaster jar... just to name a few...

Crazy, I know!

But if I'm being honest, I love that God empowered many of these prostitutes within His Kingdom. I think I love it because of how offensive it is to religious people. There is nothing quite like the Gospel spreading in a plethora of ways. Multiple puns intended...

Do you know what else is offensive to the religious? When God gives you your perfection freely as a gift.

Wait, what? I thought I fell short of His glory (insert Romans Road Bible verse). I can't possibly be perfect in the midst of my shortcomings and sin (insert your typical Sunday morning sermon).

That would be true if your perfection was based on your performance.

But what if God was waiting on humanity to wake up to a perfection they already possess because of what Jesus accomplished 2,000 years ago? If this is true, then my performance can't remove my perfection. Therefore, when God thinks about you, He sees you as complete in Christ… already perfect! These aren't my words. It's the message of Jesus!

He canceled our indebtedness (Colossians 2:14). He remembers our sins no more (Hebrews 10:17, Hebrews 8:12). Our transgressions are removed as far as the east is from the west (Psalm 103:12). John introduced Him as the "Lamb that takes away the sin of the world" in John 1:29 (not to mention that the word 'sin' is singular); and this perfected reality was prophesied by Isaiah when he said this would happen through the Messiah in Isaiah 43:25.

The only thing that isn't perfect is how you think about your perfection. Because we've been taught that it isn't humble to claim perfection, we walk around with a false humility, claiming, "I'm still in process." **But you're not in the process of becoming perfect; you're in the process of catching the revelation that you already are because of Jesus.** The only thing that is in process is your mind catching up with the reality of who you are as a son or daughter in the Kingdom of God.

The fullness of God already dwells in you. Wake up to your identity. Wake up to your perfection. Wake up to your power. This power is freely given from God, even giving us the free choice to abuse it. People recorded in Scripture abused this power in the name of God all the time... Moses, Elijah, and even my favorite Old Testament character David.

However, the power we already possess isn't to overpower people but to empower people. To help everyone understand and believe they matter. To help you and I love without limits. To help us bring Heaven to Earth. Your behavior doesn't dictate your perfection within the Kingdom of God, but it does dictate how much of the Kingdom flows through you today.

Today's Work

1. How does what you read today help conquer your negative thought from Day 1?

2. Repeat your personal motto.

3. Guided Meditation – Scan the QR Code below and watch today's video. Or visit saintsnotsinners.com and click on the 21 Day Devo tab for more information. After watching the video, I want you to come back to this page and write or draw how you feel. What do you hear, see, sense, or feel from the Spirit?

4. Today's challenge – How can you take today's devotional and encourage someone else with it?

day seventeen

. . .

Masterpiece

WHAT IF I told you God wants to show you off as His perfect masterpiece to the world?

Yesterday, we talked about perfection. I want to reiterate it for a minute because it's probably the hardest reality for us to accept. When we think about perfection, rarely do we understand the current reality of it. For the Christian, we often focus on the thought of being perfect "one day when…" Or we say, "How can I be perfect when I still sin?" The simple answer is that your perfection isn't based on your behavior. If Jesus is perfect and He lives in you, you're more perfect than you think. **Again, you're not in the process of becoming perfect; you're in the process of catching the revelation that you already are because of Jesus.**

God is the Master Painter, and He's painting expressions of Himself on your life. Ephesians 2:10 says we are God's masterpiece. The word masterpiece can be translated as handiwork or workmanship. In Greek, it's the word "poiema" where we get our English word "poem".

In other words, God wrote poetry when He spoke you into existence, for you are His beloved. You are complete and whole in Christ. You are a beautiful expression of God's brushstrokes, and He wants you to show off His perfect masterpiece!

It's inspiring to *experience* the reality of your perfection, but your perfection will be *expressed* in a specific way. In Matthew 5, Jesus says something during His sermon on the mount that many people misunderstand. We misunderstand because we don't cross-reference this passage with others like it. In verse 48, Jesus says, "Be perfect, therefore, as your heavenly Father is perfect." Many people think this is unachievable because they don't believe they're already perfect in Christ. However, 'be' is a verb of being; it is not an action verb. This is not about doing holy things. This is resting in the identity that was given to you by Jesus. But even without that knowledge, this isn't what is being communicated. In the context of this section of Jesus' sermon, He's talking about loving your enemies. I think Luke's Gospel translated what Jesus said during this moment more accurately than Matthew's. In Luke 6:36 it says, "Be merciful, just as your Father is merciful." **We experience perfection because of the performance of Jesus, yet we express perfection in our mercy and love towards humanity.** To express perfection is to be merciful. Stop trying to be 'perfect' and recognize you already are. Today, begin expressing yourself as a masterpiece of mercy to the world.

Today's Work

1. How does what you read today help conquer your negative thought from Day 1?

2. Repeat your personal motto.

3. Guided Meditation – We're going to practice sitting still today. Take 5 minutes and sit in silence. Be free of all distractions. Be quiet and take a moment to rest in God's pleasure. He delights in you. You are His masterpiece. Ask the Spirit what He thinks of you. Then, write or draw what you hear, see, sense, or feel.

4. Today's challenge – How can you take today's devotional and encourage someone else with it?

day eighteen

. . .

Saint

WHAT IF I told you you're not a sinner saved by grace but a saint saved by grace?

I heard a pastor say recently at the conclusion of his sermon, "Go tell someone you're a great sinner and then tell them about the greatness and the majesty and the forgiveness and the joy that you have because of the work and person of Jesus."

My friends, that sounds right because we've heard those types of messages our whole life, but you should never do that! Sin should never have a starring role in our Gospel presentation. And while we're on the subject, let's stop saying bull-crap things like 'hate the sin and not the sinner.' Jesus never said that. In fact, you might be shocked to find out that phrase was said by Gandhi. That phrase gives people the excuse not to love like Jesus because it screams, 'We don't love you as you are.' OR 'We'll only love you as soon as you look like us.' I find the irony in the well-meaning Christian who tries to rebuttal out of fear of condoning... as if Jesus ever worried about how others perceived His love. Jesus never called anyone a sinner because He understood that was no one's identity (don't misquote the metaphor Jesus used in Mark 2). You are not a sinner saved by grace. You are a saint saved by grace. You are a saint who still sins, but it does not define you. You are a child of God. You are His beloved. That's how you are defined!

If you need to be told how bad you are to find out how good God is, it's not the Gospel you've found. The Gospel is not an invitation to accept Jesus. It's a declaration that He has already accepted you. Once we know our permanent position, we gladly participate in the life of the Kingdom of God here on Earth now. The Gospel is the good news of the righteousness, peace, and joy we have because of Jesus. As author Danielle Shroyer says in her book *Original Blessing,* "We (unfortunately) have shifted from telling a story marked by connection to declaring a story marred by distance." She continues by saying, "God's grace can't and shouldn't be twisted and used as a way for us to feel like we're unworthy. God doesn't need to humiliate us before giving us grace just to ensure that grace is effective and appreciated. If we are told we have to feel bad before we can appreciate feeling loved, it isn't love we've found."

Again, God is a Master Painter, and He has painted you as a masterpiece (Ephesians 2:10). I like how Lecrae raps the imagery when he says, "The Master Artist makes your mess a masterpiece regardless..." That's the point of the Gospel... the good news... you are God's masterpiece. And if you are a masterpiece, you can't BE flawed. You can HAVE flaws, but that's not WHO you are. You cannot be a dirty, wretched sinner and a beloved child of God at the same time. One is a clever way the church has carried false humility for centuries... the other is your permanent identity. Sinner is not your identity. Sonship is. You're not a terrible person. You're in the process of recognizing and believing how God views you because He thinks you are amazing!

Today's Work

1. How does what you read today help conquer your negative thought from Day 1?

2. Repeat your personal motto.

3. Guided Meditation – It's time to write yourself a love letter. I know this could be weird, but it's time to affirm yourself. You get to determine the length. Tell yourself how much you love the person you are and are becoming. Make sure you use proper words, such as I am statements, aligning yourself with how the Father views you.

4. Today's challenge – How can you take today's devotional and encourage someone else with it?

day nineteen

. . .

Holy

WHAT IF I told you you can't get more holy than you already are right now?

Perfect and holy tend to be the words we have the hardest time accepting. Maybe it's because we really haven't been taught it correctly. **Holiness is not something to strive for. It's something to awaken to.** We have people striving to become holy without realizing it's a gift given to us based on the performance of Jesus, not ours. When we strive for things like this – it puts the blessings of God dependent on our obedience rather than His goodness. The goodness of God will lead you to change your mind about Him (Romans 2:4), therefore changing your mind about you. Holiness is our identity.

God says be holy, not get holy. Be holy because in Christ you already are. Which means you can't get more holy; you already are holy. Hebrews 10:10 says, "And by that will, we have been made holy through the sacrifice of the body of Jesus Christ once for all." According to the author of Hebrews, we were made holy because of the death, burial, and resurrection of Jesus. To quote Don Keathley, **"The finished work of Jesus gives us conclusions, not conditions."**

One of my favorite portions of Scripture is Colossians 1:21-22. I'm going to highlight some of the words used so you don't miss this incredible revelation.

"Once you were alienated from God and were enemies **in your minds** because of your evil behavior. But now he has reconciled you by Christ's physical body through death to present you **holy in his sight**, without blemish, and free from accusation."

You were never alienated or separated from God. How can you ever be separated from a God who is omnipresent? You only believed you were in your mind. Besides, God doesn't have any enemies. Now, because of the death, burial, and resurrection – Jesus has presented you holy in God's sight. You can reject this truth if you want, but it's only going to hinder your confidence. Either God already made you holy, or you can keep striving for something that is already yours. The choice is yours. You're holy, and there is nothing you can do about it.

Today's Work

1. How does what you read today help conquer your negative thought from Day 1?

2. Repeat your personal motto.

3. Guided Meditation – Go listen to the song "Holy of Holies" by Hill City Worship. Be free from all distractions. Be still. Either close your eyes and listen or read along with the lyrics. Which lyrics stood out the

most and why? Write or draw what you hear, see, sense, or feel from the Spirit.

Scan the QR Code below for more information or visit saintsnotsinners.com and click on the 21 Day Devo tab for more information.

4. Today's challenge – How can you take today's devotional and encourage someone else with it?

day twenty

. . .

Victorious

WHAT IF I told you living victoriously in life has everything to do with how you think about your circumstances?

Almost every time, you can trace back your heartbreaks and disappointments to a choice someone made. You may have been victimized, but you are not a victim. You may be walking through an extremely difficult season, but you are not defined by it. You can't always control what happens to you, but you can always control how you respond to what happens to you. What I want you to know today is you have full control over how you react to life. In spite of what our society says, you are not a victim. As neuroscientist Dr. Caroline Leaf says, "We are not even victims of our biology. We are co-creators of our destiny alongside God."

We need to get rid of this victim mentality and recognize our identity as children of God. We are victors! It's a common Christian cliché, but it's still true – we don't train FOR victory; we train FROM it. We must never allow our circumstances to dictate our feelings because our feelings aren't always facts. Jesus Himself was treated as a victim, but He never allowed Himself to feel and live like one. He even forgave His abusers in the midst of hanging from a tree. 'Yea but that's Jesus,' people say… Well, before Stephen was stoned to death for his faith in Acts 6-7, his last prayer wasn't for God to save him from injustice. Rather, he prayed for the forgiveness of those who were killing him. This tells us everything we need to know about his victor mentality.

Life is constantly full of tension. You are guaranteed to go through seasons of pushing and pulling, ups and downs, ebbs and flows. If we allow the constant change to discombobulate who Jesus says we are, we negate what was done on the cross 2,000 years ago. Jesus wrapped Himself in flesh to empower and transfigure us from death to life, depression to joy, anxiety to peace, victim to victor. Our circumstances only have as much power over us as we allow. We have full control over the thoughts we hold on to. We must transform the way we think about ourselves because our heavenly Father calls us whole, loved, unique, chosen, qualified, worthy, secured, accepted, valued, royal, forgiven, blameless, righteous, known, perfect, a masterpiece, a saint, and holy.

Start by speaking life over yourself and walk in your true identity as a son or daughter of God. You're a victor. You're all those words listed above. Start claiming victory in your life because Christ was and is victorious!

Today's Work

1. How does what you read today help conquer your negative thought from Day 1?

2. Repeat your personal motto.

3. Guided Meditation – Make a list and write out what you are thankful for. Again, you get to determine how long this list is and whether or not you want to keep adding to it in the future. Then, I want you to think about what is currently going on in your life. What is troubling you? What are you anxious about? Bring the thought to the surface. What is beyond your control? What is within your control? Focus on what you can control and then repeat the following – I am capable. I am victorious. I will focus on what I can control.

4. Today's challenge – How can you take today's devotional and encourage someone else with it?

day twenty one

. . .

Greatness

WHAT IF I told you God believes in you?

When you can't see the greatness you were born with, you will settle for less than your worth. **You don't give God any honor by putting yourself down.**

In Mark 10:35-45, we read James and John arguing over who is the greatest. We often miss an incredible revelation of true greatness once Jesus gets involved in the conversation. Jesus did not have a problem with their desire for greatness. He had a problem with what they thought greatness was. What's crazy is the same argument over who is the greatest happens again in Luke 22 during the last supper. Again, Jesus did not rebuke His disciples for wanting to be great. Instead, He showed them how – by washing their feet. True greatness empowers, serves, and loves others. Greatness is not about winning, controlling, or proving; it's about liberating, healing, and restoring. He showed them their perspective about greatness was jacked. Greatness in the Kingdom of God is not about climbing the ladder of success to gain a bigger title. It's about recognizing your title as a child of God and grabbing a bigger towel. When we wash feet, it's about lifting others up without putting ourselves down.

For the record, Jesus knew Judas was going to betray Him, and He still washed his feet. The test of following Jesus is not how you love Jesus – it's how you love others, especially how you love Judas.

We must understand our greatness because a great God lives in us. Greatness requires discipline, and we must kill the idea that greatness looks different than being faithful to everyday life. Greatness is simply serving and loving others from the overflow of being served and loved by God. Greatness is in you, but it's expressed by serving and loving your spouse, kids, parents, friends, etc. Being great is recognizing that 'normal' is okay. Being great is being a present spouse and parent. Being great is looking out for your friends and rejoicing at their success while also being a shoulder to lean on in their failures. Being great is about doing the millions of small things that bring accomplishment into the picture. Being great starts when you stop striving for a position you already have. Being great is recognizing how much God believes in you.

Being great is not about following Jesus to get into Heaven. It's about bringing Heaven to Earth! It's about recognizing you have the power to bring Heaven into every room you walk into.

Today's Work

1. How does what you read today help conquer your negative thought from Day 1?

2. Repeat your personal motto.

3. Guided Meditation – Go listen to the song "Heaven Is Everywhere" by Johnnyswim. Be free from all distractions. Be still. Either close your eyes and listen or read along with the lyrics. Which lyrics stood out the most and why? Write or draw what you hear, see, sense, or feel from the Spirit.

Scan the QR Code below for more information or visit saintsnotsinners.com and click on the 21 Day Devo tab for more information.

4. Today's challenge – How can you take today's devotional and encourage someone else with it?

last challenge

. . .

CONGRATULATIONS! You should be very proud of yourself. How does it feel to talk differently to yourself? You did the work. You were honest. You're beginning to see how amazing you are, and everyone in your circle will reap the benefits because of your hard work. As I shared in the word of caution, a lack of confidence is a bad habit that takes time to break. Scientifically, according to clinical and cognitive neuroscientist Dr. Caroline Leaf – it takes 63 days (or three cycles of 21 days. Which is why this devotional is 21 days) to break down a habit or pattern of thinking. It only takes 1 cycle of 21 days to break down a core habit and build a replacement one. (To avoid falling back into the habit or thought pattern, it's recommended to continue through two more cycles). It takes time to retrain your brain about how to think about yourself. This work is not about intensity; it's about consistency. Consistently speaking God's truth into your soul. So, I challenge you to go through this devotional again. Pick a new negative thought that you struggle with and begin to conquer it.

about the author

Cory Rice is is the Teaching Pastor and part of the counseling team at Hill City Church, located in Southern Indiana near Louisville, Kentucky. He is co-host *of 2 Pastors And A Mic PODCAST*. He's a husband, father, and the author of *Jailbreak*, *Stoker*, and *Transitioned*. He is married to an incredible Ukrainian babe, Julia, who was rescued from the orphan system. Together they are raising three children: Henry, Scarlett, and Zion. Cory has received three masters and is currently working on his doctorate from Global Grace Seminary. He's a washed- up hockey player who loves all things sports, trash-talk, good coffee, guacamole, and Air Jordan shoes.

You can learn more about Cory at saintsnotsinners.com

also by cory rice

These books are available on Amazon and can also be purchased through Cory's website: saintsnotsinners.com

Jail Break: Escaping Illusion, Discovering Sonship, Living Free

Stoker

Transitioned